T0365337

a little blessing

haiku and photography by william duke

Library of Congress Control Number: 2015914145

ISBN: Softcover   978-1-5144-0177-4
        Hardcover   978-1-5144-0179-8
        EBook   978-1-5144-0178-1

Print information available on the last page.

Rev. date: 09/25/2015

To order additional copies of this book, contact:
Xlibris
1-888-795-4274
www.Xlibris.com
Orders@Xlibris.com

Preface

In early July of 2014, I attended Steve Earle's Camp Copperhead in Big Indian, New York. At the camp, Steve discussed how the daily practice of haiku writing was suggested to him by Michael Stipe of REM. Steve took up the challenge and showed us his Word document of a full year of poems to prove it!

Haiku is a poetic form calling for three lines: first five syllables, second seven syllables, and then five syllables. The subject is nature and it should reflect the seasons without specifically mentioning fall winter or spring.

On the morning we left camp, the mist was burning off the mountains and I snapped a photo for Facebook. The beauty of the landscape inspired my first poem and I made a commitment to write one every day with a photograph for a full year.

The Art Now movement of Peter Mayer insists that the artist engages in his or her craft on a regular basis. This strong bias toward action has many benefits when applied to poetry. Giving myself a daily assignment helped free my imagination and force me to be more present and open to nature throughout the day. The act of writing the poem was also a daily meditation. Please enjoy the pictures and the poems in this book. Each one is "a little blessing" for me.

Acknowledgments

I'd like to thank all of my Facebook friends who provided encouragement every day of the year by "liking" and commenting on my daily entries.

Jay Merwin was also helpful looking over the work. His insightful comments informed the selection of poems and accompanying photos for the book.

Finally, I'd like to thank my wife, Madonna Badger, who designed a beautiful layout for the book. She was also very encouraging and only occasionally raised her eyebrows at the sight of her husband mumbling to himself while counting syllables on his fingers.

July 10

Mist burns off the mountain;
dreams may come real today;
birds say good morning.

July 11

Morning sun rises
over Gladstone Valley Road.
Frog finally rests.

July 12

Weeds in the driveway
dig deep roots through crusher rock.
Must have a purpose.

July 19

Lilies do no not care
if sky is cloudy or dark.
Perhaps the frogs do.

July 26

Daybreak on Hyzer Hill
birds form their jazz ensemble.
Free-flowing. Awake.

July 27

Milk cows coming in
don't worry about being
heavy on the hoof.

July 28

Fresh-picked wildflowers
from the side of the driveway.
I'm told they are weeds.

July 29

Fat hydrangea
makes the hosta look forlorn.
No comparison.

July 31

Bee and sunflower
will always need each other.
It seems we do too.

Aug 4

Mushrooms have come up
after last night's strong rain.
A little blessing.

Aug 5

Weeds grow high again
where lawnmowers go to die.
Always samsara.

August 6

The pretty thistle
will stand alone on the bank
dying to be picked.

Aug 8

The birds understand
why the pretty little fruit
is so becoming.

Aug 11

The exhausted nymph
finds warm sun and compassion.
It may fly again.

Aug 12

Morning rain comes, goes.
My footprints dry on the porch.
The grass grows greener.

8

Aug 14

The puzzled sheep stare
at the man filled with promise
to write this morning.

Aug 15

The little nymph died:
soon to be something else.
See the potato.

Aug 17

The startled serpent
Freezes by its rocky nest.
Hawk circles above.

9

Aug 20

This stone grey morning
climbing on an iron gate
rose buds die and bloom.

Aug 22

Tomatos hang low;
blueberries ripen in field.
Bird house empty.

Aug 22

Grey morning, ragweed.
The bride prepares to marry.
Love always abides.

Aug 23

Streams come together
underneath a rusty bridge.
Leaves float down river.

Aug 25

As the fog burns off
The drunkard finally gives up.
The swing hangs empty.

Aug 26

Misplaced grasshopper
feeds a hungry camera.
Zero calories.

Sept 1

Red roses open.
The blue bottle is empty.
They cannot compare.

Sept 2

Stillness everywhere,
yet the pond may be disturbed.
The fly beats its wings.

Sept 4

The sky's reflection
drifting slowly on surface
past the grass and tree.

12

Sept 6

Feathery knotweed
flowers know no boundaries:
Globalization.

Sept 8

The beech tree losing
its leaves. More each day.
Nothing can be done.

Sept 10

The rain's dying down.
The harvestman still awaits
the warming sunshine.

13

Sept 17

Hydrangia turns
dark. There's a chill in the air.
The crows are busy.

Sept 19

Finding way back home
over mountains of desire
to the quiet place.

Sept 20th

Beneath golden sea
some find a point where all is
deserving of love.

Sept 22

The wide road curves
through dark valley of the trees,
leading toward the light.

Sept 25

Way out in distance
beyond the rocks and maples
a man climbs steep path.

Sept 26

Sweet abandonment;
letting go, understanding
entropy prevails.

Oct 2

Winding mountain road,
welcoming on shady day,
but beware deer.

Oct 4

On a high pasture
blue sky and milkweed
celebrate their love.

Oct 6

Milkweed cracks open
spreading it's seed in the grass:
Dying to give birth.

Oct 8

Sun setting sooner;
Sumac shedding crimson coat.
Songbirds have left us.

Oct 11

Peeling paint in sun;
mice returning from the fields.
Finding acceptance.

Oct 12

This morning's woodstove
cooking like there's no tomorrow;
but there always is.

Oct 14

There's a chill in air
when we lose someone we love.
Grey lake mirrors sky.

Oct 15

The canopy's thick
so we cannot see the sky.
But we know it's there.

Oct 16

Visiting with past
let conversation slow down.
The barn's still breathing.

Oct 17

In another time
reflection, stillness, beauty
following one breath.

Oct 18

Mountains are moving
like waves upon the ocean
with slower motion.

Oct 20

Sumac's last sad fronds
remain after first snowfall;
wind is coming soon.

19

Oct 21

Reservoir falling;
the rocky shores widening
pastures from the past.

Oct 23

Raccoon in headlights;
fugitive loose in mountains;
fear rises, rain falls.

Oct 24

Fat sheep now grazing;
grass is green and plentiful.
They have no judgment.

Oct 25

An empty storefront
basks in the late-day sunshine.
Beckoning, lonely.

Oct 26

Taste Blues, Reds, Russets,
Carollas and Fingerlings.
Variety Rocks!

Oct 28

Now leaves have fallen
revealing the cold hard truth:
The nest is empty.

Oct 30

Basking on the ridge
old barn at Sunny Slope Farm--
is still becoming.

Nov 2

Goldenrod's white ghost.
Coyotes howl. Rabbits run.
All souls understand.

Nov 3

Snow dusts the valley.
Leaves on lilac tree remain
in cold denial.

Nov 4

Strong timber standing
on the crest of Cabin Hill
one day at a time.

Nov 7

Highland pastures gone.
Lichen thrives on grey stone wall:
Perhaps place to sit.

Nov 13

The golden hour
when stream releases secret
source of all beauty.

Nov. 14

The wide river flows
in and out and up and down,
as though it's breathing.

Nov 15

Down beyond the bend
the cold road must be lonely
silent and serene.

Nov 16

Thin ice covers pond;
lilies become palimpsest.
Nature now sleeps.

Nov 17

Across the valley
the cracking sound of gunshots,
changing perspective.

Nov 19

Ancestor's planter
lost in an abandoned field:
Free from attachment.

Nov 22

The road twists and turns.
Find at the end of the day
where you're meant to be.

Nov 23

Life, death, snow, rocks, earth,
connected to the Devine
nature in all things.

Nov 35

Dog's kill now frozen.
One eye reflects long shadows,
bare maple, crow, sky.

Nov 30

Upon reflection
nothing is just black or white;
just soft wash of grey.

Dec 2

Breaking over hills
see breathtaking reminder
we are still alive.

Dec 8

A full moon rises
above long low reservoir.
Deer run on dark side.

Dec 16

At end of the day
a dead fish lies on the ice,
ready for dinner.

Dec 21

On the shortest day
find sun barely appearing
beyond low dark clouds.

Jan 13

Dawn comes in silence.
Snow lays down its comforter.
Friends have flown away.

Jan 16

Now she stands naked,
balancing effort and ease,
bright sun and shadow.

Jan 17

Epiphany comes
when light fades over the hill;
dusk brings the cold truth.

Jan 18

Stillness in the air
hangs over the frozen pond;
a frog music rest.

Jan 19

Voice cries out softly
from woods of isolation:
Please repair our bridge!

Jan 20

Any road will do.
Even if it's familiar,
love the scenery.

Jan 21

Powder white pasture,
open to a cloudy sky,
accepting more snow

Jan 22

Cold tributary
runs in every direction;
finds easiest course.

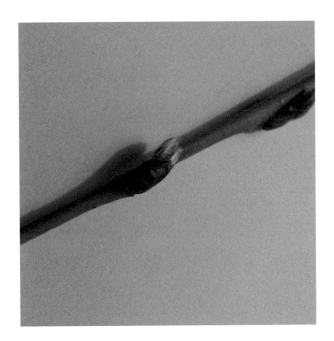

Jan 23

Our willow begins
budding in cold longer days;
prana unfolding.

Jan 24

Under mackerel sky
mountain magic may move us
close to the Divine.

Jan 26

Liquid turns solid;
warm day and cold night create
new states of matter.

Jan 30

Soft pink morning sky
tells us everything we need,
if we can listen.

Jan 31

Snow-covered cow stares
into storm. Insulated,
warm on the inside.

Feb 5

Ice flows down river;
sumac clings to snowy cliff;
still sunset dissolves.

Feb 6

Puddles turn to ice.
Ducks drop ego and judgment;
share some Cheerios.

Feb 7

Dark angry apples
reach towards the evening sky;
waiting for songbirds.

Feb 8

Soft morning sun climbs
over hills, through cloudy sky,
shines on every road.

Feb 16

Frightened birds alight
into the windy snow fall.
Dogs scratch on car door.

Feb 17

Mind numbing deep freeze;
nature abhors a vacuum;
somewhere a bird calls.

Feb 18

Sun flashes on snow;
chickadee flies inside house;
woodpile's almost gone.

Feb 19

Crow flies over snow;
searching the frozen valley;
frog sleeps safe in pond.

Feb 21

White birch stems divide,
rooting beside frozen stream;
pain is a teacher.

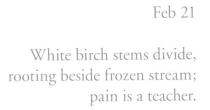

Feb 22

Knee deep in the snow
covering pastures of plenty,
stag longs for the stream.

Feb 24

Wind whistles through trees.
The crow climbs over valley;
below, cold stream flows.

Feb 28

Dogs pad around room;
pipes knock as the heat comes up.
Now meditation.

Mar 1

Longer days are here.
The sun shines off the snow piles;
bright cold reflection.

March 2

Bare trees stand like ghosts;
empty birdhouse waits alone;
breath floats in cold air.

Mar 3

Snow lies wet and deep;
no tracks or trail lead the way
to understanding.

Mar 8

The junco's hopping
slowly across crusty snow.
No dog can catch it.

Mar 9

Violet clouds drift
behind the darkening hills;
present becomes past.

March 10

The chickadee sits
feeding on seed as snow melts
into afternoon.

March 13

Wind whistles through trees.
The stone church stands unmoving.
Ice cracks on river.

March 15

Fawns gambol on edge
of pasture. Grazing on brush
and hay in round bales.

March 17

Sheep stand on parade;
thick winter wool keeps them warm.
Top of the morning!

March 18

The bright light breaks through;
reality apparent
when seen by one man.

March 20

Man pets his prized boar
which will sire sixty hogs;
Now that's food for thought!

March 21

Deer find a bare patch
to graze on in the snowfield;
grateful for warm sun.

March 22

Temperature climbs.
wood lies open in truck bed
waiting to be stacked.

March 23

The golden moment
when again the sun comes up
over fallen snow.

March 24

The general store
stocks all of our essentials;
everything changes.

March 31

Old retaining wall
supports the snowy hillside.
Lichen thrives on stone.

April 5

Stream swells with snow melt;
the full moon begins to wane;
frozen land lets go.

April 6

More snow falls again,
melting as fast as it lands.
Boots sink deep in mud.

April 8

Blackbird calls from tree;
warm rain falls on crusty snow;
rhododendron buds.

April 11

Ice melts on the pond;
the ground begins to soften;
frogs may now wake up.

April 12

Desiccated cat
surveys sculptor's studio;
silent sentinel.

April 13

Beaver basks in stream;
gnawed branch lies on shoreline;
Both may change the world.

April 14

By dark muddy path
mushroom grows on rotten tree.
The warm sun returns.

April 15

Resting on water,
lost in the sky's reflection,
two geese move as one.

April 23

Wet road shines silver,
running west into hollow.
Frogs sing once again.

April 24

Sheep stares like a ghost
asking directions in dream.
There is no reply.

May 3

Through lilac curtain
full moon waltzes over hills.
Crickets orchestrate.

May 4

Trout lily appears
before us on forest floor.
Other herbs follow.

May 6

High on sylvan hill
old leaves tremble on white beech;
spirits in the wind.

May 9

Suddenly they've come;
dandelions flower, grow
leaves for a salad.

May 10

New leaf of willow
greets paddlers down west branch
looking for some shade.

May 12

Apple blossoms, now
fragrance fills evening air;
dreams have become real.

May 13

Rain stops. Rainbow comes.
Over lush green grassy slope,
wet dogwood bows down.

May 14

Hummingbird hovers;
wings beat faster than the eye;
longing for nectar.

May 15

Startled chipmunk stares
at blue jay landing on lawn
to join him for lunch.

May 16

Robin surveys hillside;
three blue eggs lie in a nest,
wait for her return.

May 17

Startled drake takes off,
flies over silver surface;
cattails undisturbed.

May 18

The painting begins;
new colors on the canvas,
and everywhere else.

May 19

Sun comes up before
fog burns off of the valley.
Someone is watching.

May 22

The woodpecker drums
into the large lilac branch;
Nature can play jazz.

May 24

The mourning dove lands
next to the redwing blackbird;
both share abundance.

May 25

Spider climbs column
slowly. Waiting in sunshine.
Patience has rewards.

May 26

Dandelions turn
white, stems carpet the pasture,
waiting for the wind.

May 28

Solitary drake
swimming circles in the pond;
rain is on the way.

May 29

Blackbird calls again,
protecting its willow tree;
hoping for a mate.

June 2

The round bales are green;
lie on the freshly cut field;
smell of sweet decay.

June 4

John Burroughs lived
to observe and to record
nature every day.

June 9

Beavers at work;
stream now still pond of water
above the pasture.

June 10

Field flowers arise;
globe amaranth, butter cup
have their time in sun.

June 11

The lavender light
fades behind the tall hemlocks
so we see the moon.

June 12

Snake basks on warm rock;
metabolism heats up;
waiting for a mouse.

June 13

Porcupine decays;
carrion feeds bugs and worms
which may feed the birds.

June 14

See fresh free range eggs
with subtle and sublime hue;
tan, brown, green and blue.

June 15

Iris open up;
bloom now next to stone wall.
Soon the rain will come.

June 16

Broken window shows
sad season of disrepair.
The doves nest inside.

June 17

Paint cracks off wet wood;
old house shows signs of neglect.
Sun will come out soon.

June 18

Chicks chirp together
strutting under the warm lamp.
The dog goes crazy.

June 21

Water rushes down
Insane stream in longest day.
Every leaf is open.

June 23

Days are shorter now;
Experience recommends love;
golden times flowing.

June 24

Lambs graze on long grass;
some lost in the lush landscape.
Here today, gone soon.

June 26

Beyond the dark clouds,
on way to bright open sky;
lights shine on wet road.

56

June 27

Moth lands on flower;
morning dew evaporates;
fields smell like cut hay.

June 28

Mixed greens in raised bed;
growing kale, spinach, swiss shard;
scrumptious salad soon.

June 30

Day lilies blooming;
one stem follows another;
each has time in sun.

July 2

The path runs between
two trees. Follow it to find
sheep lost in high grass.

July 3

Evening slowly falls
over green fields and blue hills;
Gladstone Valley rests.

July 4

Clouds cover the sky;
Hills recede in the distance;
Blackbird awakens.

July 5

Catskill crowd parties,
fireworks fill the valley,
echo off the hills.

July 6

A confused deer stands
frozen on the road's shoulder;
drivers must take care.

July 7

Golden sun rises;
dew burns off the growing grass;
spider spins her web.

July 9

Private property
posted onto the tree trunk;
woodpeckers care less.

July 10

Wildflowers border
sunny road and dappled wood.
Every day they bloom.

July 11

Wild berries ripen;
no vine grows to heaven
and everything ends.

July 12

Caterpillar walks;
The leaf trembles in the wind;
Change can be painful.

A resident of both New York City and Andes, New York, William Duke is a gardener, poet, singer songwriter, painter, yoga instructor and real estate broker. His daily practice of writing haiku combined with a smart phone photograph is documented in social media posts, taking us through a full year of pronounced seasons in Catskills. Through this work, Duke shares a keen, exciting, spiritual, and loving view of the natural world.

Printed in the United States
By Bookmasters